U.S.NRC

United States Nuclear Regulatory Commission

Protecting People and the Environment

I0413521

NUREG-1830,
Volume 8
February 2012

FY 2011 USNRC | OFFICE OF INVESTIGATIONS

AVAILABILITY OF REFERENCE MATERIALS
IN NRC PUBLICATIONS

NRC Reference Material

As of November 1999, you may electronically access NUREG-series publications and other NRC records at NRC=s Public Electronic Reading Room at http://www.nrc.gov/reading-rm.html.
Publicly released records include, to name a few, NUREG-series publications; *Federal Register* notices; applicant, licensee, and vendor documents and correspondence; NRC correspondence and internal memoranda; bulletins and information notices; inspection and investigative reports; licensee event reports; and Commission papers and their attachments.

NRC publications in the NUREG series, NRC regulations, and *Title 10, Energy*, in the Code of *Federal Regulations* may also be purchased from one of these two sources.
1. The Superintendent of Documents
   U.S. Government Printing Office
   Mail Stop SSOP
   Washington, DC 20402B0001
   Internet: bookstore.gpo.gov
   Telephone: 202-512-1800
   Fax: 202-512-2250
2. The National Technical Information Service
   Springfield, VA 22161B0002
   www.ntis.gov
   1B800B553B6847 or, locally, 703B605B6000

A single copy of each NRC draft report for comment is available free, to the extent of supply, upon written request as follows:
Address:　U.S. Nuclear Regulatory Commission
　　　　　　 Office of Administration
　　　　　　 Publications Branch
　　　　　　 Washington, DC 20555-0001
E-mail:　　 DISTRIBUTION.SERVICES@NRC.GOV
Facsimile:　301B415B2289

Some publications in the NUREG series that are posted at NRC=s Web site address http://www.nrc.gov/reading-rm/doc-collections/nuregs are updated periodically and may differ from the last printed version. Although references to material found on a Web site bear the date the material was accessed, the material available on the date cited may subsequently be removed from the site.

Non-NRC Reference Material

Documents available from public and special technical libraries include all open literature items, such as books, journal articles, and transactions, *Federal Register* notices, Federal and State legislation, and congressional reports. Such documents as theses, dissertations, foreign reports and translations, and non-NRC conference proceedings may be purchased from their sponsoring organization.

Copies of industry codes and standards used in a substantive manner in the NRC regulatory process are maintained atc
　　The NRC Technical Library
　　Two White Flint North
　　11545 Rockville Pike
　　Rockville, MD 20852B2738

These standards are available in the library for reference use by the public. Codes and standards are usually copyrighted and may be purchased from the originating organization or, if they are American National Standards, fromc
　　American National Standards Institute
　　11 West 42nd Street
　　New York, NY 10036B8002
　　www.ansi.org
　　212B642B4900

Legally binding regulatory requirements are stated only in laws; NRC regulations; licenses, including technical specifications; or orders, not in NUREG-series publications. The views expressed in contractor-prepared publications in this series are not necessarily those of the NRC.

The NUREG series comprises (1) technical and administrative reports and books prepared by the staff (NUREGBXXXX) or agency contractors (NUREG/CRBXXXX), (2) proceedings of conferences (NUREG/CPBXXXX), (3) reports resulting from international agreements (NUREG/IABXXXX), (4) brochures (NUREG/BRBXXXX), and (5) compilations of legal decisions and orders of the Commission and Atomic and Safety Licensing Boards and of Directors= decisions under Section 2.206 of NRC=s regulations (NUREGB0750).

ABSTRACT

This report provides the Commission with an overview of the U.S. Nuclear Regulatory Commission's Office of Investigations (OI) activities, mission, and purpose, along with the framework of case inventory with highlights of significant cases completed by OI during Fiscal Year 2011 (Staff Requirements Memorandum COMJC898, dated June 30, 1989). This is the 23rd OI annual report.

CONTENTS

FISCAL YEAR 2011 HIGHLIGHTS

During Fiscal Year (FY) 2011, the U.S. Nuclear Regulatory Commission's (NRC's) Office of Investigations (OI) maintained a missiondriven, highperforming, resultsfocused workforce that enhanced its dedication to effective communication and stakeholder outreach. OI comprises experienced Federal criminal investigators and a professional administrative support staff. The OI staff is continuously motivated to exceed the expectations of both internal and external stakeholders while increasing opportunities for operational awareness, engagement, empowerment, and the open exchange of ideas in accomplishing OI's role within the NRC's mission.

- OI accomplished the following significant achievements during FY 2011:

- OI closed 121 investigations. Ninetyseven percent of these investigations developed sufficient information to reach a substantiated or unsubstantiated conclusion of willful wrongdoing, thus exceeding OIs performance goal of 90 percent.

- Of the 117 investigations that OI closed with sufficient information to reach a conclusion (substantiated or unsubstantiated) of willful wrongdoing, 85 percent were closed in 9 months or less. OI's performance exceeded the goal of 80 percent for reactor investigations and met the goal of 85 percent for materials investigations.

- OI completed 100 percent of the 59 Assists to the NRC Staff that it closed within 90 days, thus exceeding its performance goal of 90 percent.

- OI processed, in a timely manner, 55 actions resulting from Freedom of Information Act requests during FY 2011.

- OI referred 100 percent of its substantiated wrongdoing investigations to the U.S. Department of Justice (DOJ) to be considered for prosecution.

- OI maintained continued awareness of emerging issues, specifically those involving Title 10 of the Code of Federal Regulations (10 CFR) Part 110, "Export and Import of Nuclear Equipment and Material." OI substantiated the allegation that CPN International, Inc. (CPN) willfully exported, and willfully attempted to export, moisture density equipment (nuclear gauges) to embargoed destinations in violation of NRC regulations.

- OI continues to provide investigative and law enforcement expertise in the development and implementation of the counterfeit, fraudulent, and suspect item (CFSI) initiative, including the appointment of a dedicated CFSI lead agent who routinely attends quarterly Washington, DC, Counterfeit Microelectronics Working Group meetings; participates and represents OI at the NRC's CFSI Steering Group meetings; and seeks membership in Operation Guardian and Operation Chain Reaction.

- OI continues to ensure that its cadre of special agents receives timely, useful, and quality training as provided by the Federal Law Enforcement Training Center. This training includes, but is not limited to, quarterly firearms training, law enforcement control techniques, and decisions of the U.S. Supreme Court and the U.S. Circuit Court pertinent to all Federal law enforcement officers.

- OI: Headquarters hosted a joint meeting coordinated by OI, Region II and Region IV designed to increase communication, cooperation, and operational awareness of emerging import/export issues. The meeting was attended by OI personnel, the NRC staff, and various Federal law enforcement agencies.

- OI continues to participate in the Federal Bureau of Investigation Counterterrorism Working Group and to provide support to the group on items of mutual interest. OI agents have gained outstanding support and cooperation from Federal and State law enforcement agencies by routinely attending Anti-Terrorism Advisory Council meetings.

- A former security officer (SO) at Arkansas Nuclear One (ANO) provided the NRC with information and photographs alleging widespread inattentiveness by the security force officers at ANO. Within 12 hours of receiving the allegation, OI initiated investigative activities, and a team of agents responded to ANO. Within 7 days, the agents had interviewed the majority of security personnel. OI's rapid and effective response ensured that the NRC had timely and preliminary information as to whether the alleged inattentiveness was widespread and/or ongoing. The investigation is continuing.

- OI continue to provide fingerprinting expertise in support of agency reinvestigations and security background clearances for current NRC employees and contractors.

With an eye toward continuous process improvement while working collaboratively with the Office of Information Services and the Computer Security Office staff and in an effort to achieve greater efficiency, all OI transitioned to the use of mobile desktop computers. These computers enable OI personnel to efficiently access the OI management information system and, consequently, investigative case file information, from remote locations.

INTRODUCTION AND OVERVIEW

MISSION AND AUTHORITY

As stated in the NRC's Strategic Plan for FY 2008–2013, the NRC's mission is to license and regulate the Nation's civilian use of byproduct, source, and special nuclear materials to ensure adequate protection of public health and safety, to promote the common defense and security, and to protect the environment. The NRC's vision is excellence in regulating the safe and secure use and management of radioactive materials for the public good. The mission and vision provide the framework for the agency's strategies and goals, which in turn guide the allocation of resources across the agency.

OI aligns with the agency's regulatory programs and strategic values and goals to provide for the safe use of radioactive materials and nuclear fuels for beneficial civilian purposes that are enabled by the agency's adherence to the principles of good regulatory independence, openness, efficiency, clarity, and reliability and by its issuance of regulatory actions that are effective, realistic, and timely.

The Commission has delegated to the OI Director the authority to take the necessary steps to accomplish the OI mission, as described in 10 CFR 1.36, "Office of Investigations," issued in 1998. See Section 161(c) of the Atomic Energy Act of 1954, as amended (42 U.S.C. § 2201(c)) and Section 206 of the Energy Reorganization Act of 1974 (42 U.S.C. § 5846). OI's investigative jurisdiction extends to the investigation of alleged wrongdoing by licensees, certificate holders, permit holders, or applicants; by contractors, subcontractors, and vendors of such entities; and by management, supervisors, and other employed personnel of such entities who may have committed violations of the Atomic Energy Act and the Energy Reorganization Act and of rules, orders, and license conditions issued by the Commission thereunder.

Additionally, during the course of an investigation, OI may uncover potentially safetysignificant issues that may or may not be related to wrongdoing. In these instances, OI provides this information to the technical staff in a timely manner for appropriate action. OI also provides professional investigative support to the NRC staff when requested in the form of Assists to the NRC Staff. Generally, these Assists to the NRC Staff are associated with matters of regulatory concern for which the staff has requested OI investigative expertise but which do not initially involve a specific indication of wrongdoing.

THE OFFICE OF INVESTIGATIONS

The OI Director reports to the Deputy Executive Director for Materials, Waste, Research, State, Tribal, and Compliance Programs and provides investigative support to operating reactors, new reactors, and nuclear material users programs.

OI is an independent national investigations program that consists of four regionally based field offices headed by field office directors who report to OI senior management staff located at OI Headquarters. At the conclusion of FY 2011, OI had 32 special agents (Job Series GG1811 Federal Criminal Investigators) and 8 professional operational support staff members nationwide.

All NRC OI special agents have extensive backgrounds and experience in Federal criminal investigations. During FY 2011, the professional cadre of OI special agents possessed an average of 20 years of Federal law enforcement service, having previously served at various Federal agencies, including other Federal law enforcement agencies, such as the Bureau of Alcohol, Tobacco, Firearms, and Explosives; Defense Criminal Investigative Service; U.S. Naval Criminal Investigative Service; Federal Bureau of Investigation; U.S. Secret Service; U.S. Customs and Border Protection; Drug Enforcement Administration; and various offices of the inspector general. Many special agents have extensive experience in white collar crime and financial fraud investigations.

OI conducts and plans investigations of allegations of potential wrongdoing to determine willful or deliberate violations. OI conducts investigations in accordance with guidelines established by the Council of Inspectors General on Integrity and Efficiency, formerly the President's Council on Integrity and Efficiency Quality Standards for Investigations.

OI develops and implements policies, procedures, and quality control standards for investigations of licensees and applicants, and of their contractors or vendors. OI conducts and supervises investigations of allegations of wrongdoing by persons or entities within the NRC's jurisdiction and maintains proactive investigative and liaison efforts with other Federal, State, and local law enforcement officials.

DIRECTOR AND FIELD OFFICE REVIEW VISITS

The OI Director or Deputy Director, or both, annually visit each of the four OI field offices,

co-located with the four NRC regional offices. During these visits, particular emphasis is placed on enhancing effective communications among OI staff and internal stakeholders. The Director's visits include individual meetings with each OI employee to discuss a variety of subjects and to effectively address any concerns or questions. Additionally, OI Headquarters operations and support staff may accompany the OI Director during visits to OI field offices, which provide opportunities for effective knowledge transfer and increased operational and programmatic awareness. The OI Director also initiates meetings with the Regional Administrator or the Deputy Regional Administrator, to engage in constructive dialogue to continually improve stakeholder communication. These visits are intended to facilitate, encourage, and demonstrate open exchanges of ideas and expressions of differing views between OI senior management, its field office staff, and NRC regional senior management.

During field office review visits (FORV), a team conducts annual selfassessments of each OI field office to support the goal of continuous improvement of the OI national investigations program. The OI FORV team assesses three major focus areas: operations, management, and administration.

Each FORV includes a meeting of field office staff to discuss current OI Headquarters initiatives and activities, policy and procedural focus, and special or regional items of interest. In addition, the FORV team interviews OI personnel during the conduct of selfassessments to obtain timely feedback on operational or other concerns and on any issues of particular concern to the employee. Additionally, the FORV team meets with internal stakeholders, the Regional or Deputy Regional Administrator, Regional Counsel, the Enforcement Coordinator, the Office Allegation Coordinator, and any other regional staff deemed appropriate. These meetings are designed to solicit stakeholder input on the effectiveness of OI's support and to improve the quality, effectiveness, and efficiency of OI's performance.

At the conclusion of the FORVs, the team conducts exit briefings with OI Field Office Directors and OI staff to discuss its findings and recommendations. OI senior management and the OI Headquarters staff conduct a final review of the FORV team's findings to identify and implement best practices with a view toward continuous process improvement.

CASES

CASE INVENTORY

Figure 1 shows the OI case inventory, which includes all investigations and Assists to the NRC Staff conducted during the FYs indicated. Figure 1 includes cases carried over from the previous year and those opened in the current year. Generally, Assists to the NRC Staff are matters of regulatory concern for which the staff has requested OI investigative expertise but which may not involve specific indications of wrongdoing. The total case inventory in FY 2011 was 298. This total case inventory includes 227 investigations, 99 of which were carried over from FY 2010. It also includes 71 Assists to the NRC Staff, 9 of which were carried over from FY 2010. The total number of cases in the OI inventory during FY 2011 was 298, which is an 8percent decrease from 325 in FY 2010.

FIGURE 1 OI CASE INVENTORY

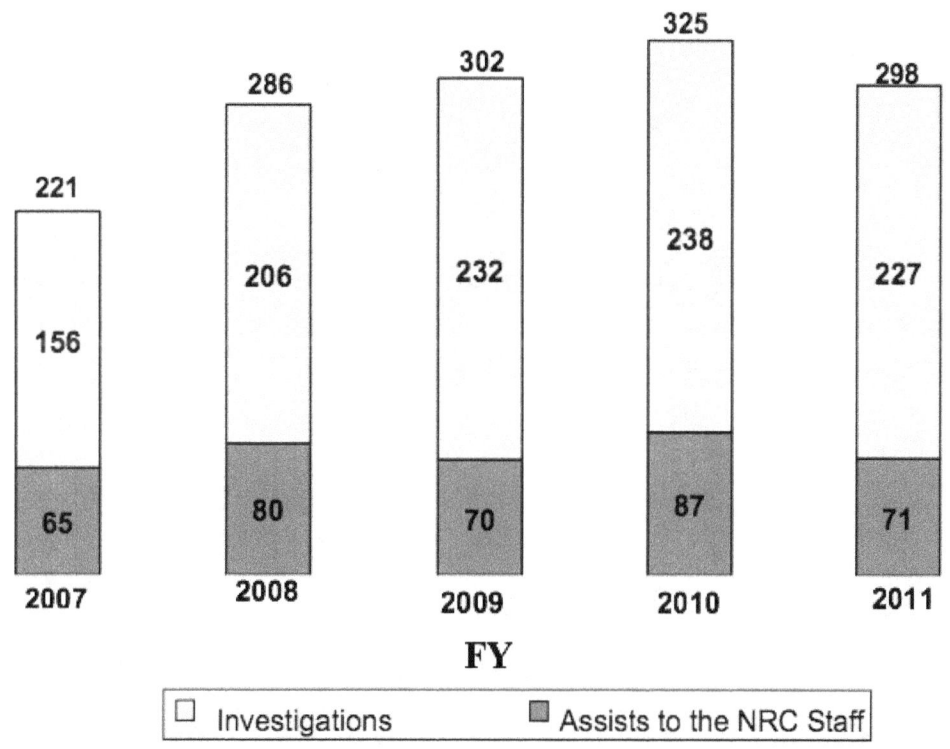

CASES OPENED

Table 1 shows the number of cases that were opened by category during FY 2007–2011.

In FY 2011, the total number of cases opened from FY 2010 decreased by 13 percent. The number of suspected material false statement cases decreased by 29 percent, and the number of violations of other NRC regulatory requirements decreased by 13 percent. In FY 2011, the number of discrimination investigations increased by 15 percent, and the number of Assists to the NRC Staff cases decreased by 24 percent. OI opened 199 cases in FY 2011, as shown in the categories listed in Table 1.

TABLE 1 CASES OPENED BY CATEGORY*

CATEGORY	FY 2007	FY 2008	FY 2009	FY 2010	FY 2011
Material false statements	17	21	23	21	15
Violations of other NRC regulatory requirements	66	97	86	79	69
Discrimination	25	32	30	46	53
Assists to the NRC Staff	62	72	67	82	62
Total	170	222	206	228	199

* Note that, of the 199 cases opened in FY 2011, 8 percent were material false statements, 35 percent were violations of other NRC regulatory requirements, 27 percent were discrimination cases, and 31 percent were Assists to the NRC Staff.

Figure 2 shows the distribution of cases that were opened during FY 2007–2011 for the reactor and materials programs. From FY 2010 to FY 2011, the overall number of (Reactor investigations and Reactor Assists to the NRC Staff) decreased by 2 percent with a 5 percent increase in reactor investigations and a 17 percent decrease in reactorrelated Assists to the NRC Staff. Materials investigations and Materials Assists to the NRC Staff, decreased overall by 42 percent with a 43 percent decrease in materials investigations and a 42 percent decrease in materialsrelated Assists to the NRC Staff.

FIGURE 2 CASES OPENED DURING FY 2007–2011 FOR THE REACTOR AND MATERIALS PROGRAMS

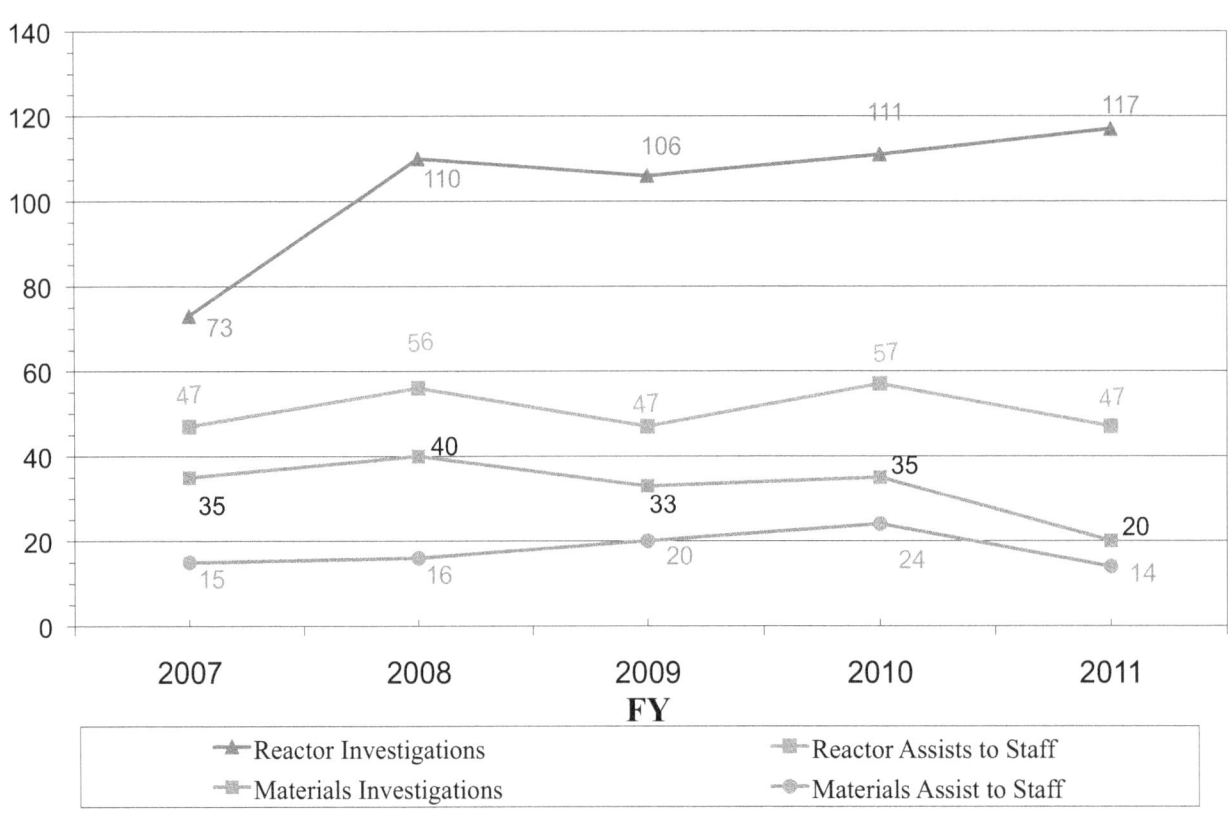

CASES CLOSED

Table 2 shows the number of cases that were closed by category during FY 2007–2011. The total cases that were closed during FY 2011 represent a 20percent decrease from the number closed in FY 2010. Material false statements investigations decreased by 42 percent, and investigations involving violations of other NRC regulatory requirements decreased by 10 percent. Discrimination investigations decreased by 21 percent, and Assists to the NRC Staff decreased by 24 percent. OI closed 180 cases in FY 2011, as shown in the categories listed in Table 2.

TABLE 2 CASES CLOSED BY CATEGORY*

CATEGORY	FY 2007	FY 2008	FY 2009	FY 2010	FY 2011
Material false statements	10	12	23	21	12
Violations of other NRC regulatory requirements	59	77	90	85	76
Discrimination	30	25	27	42	33
Assists to the NRC Staff	57	77	65	78	59
Total	156	191	205	226	180

* Note that, of the 180 cases closed in FY 2011, 7 percent were material false statements, 42 percent were violations of other NRC regulatory requirements, 18 percent were discrimination, and 33 percent were Assists to the NRC Staff.

Figure 3 shows the cases that were closed during FY 2007–2011 for reactor and materials programs. From FY 2010 to FY 2011, the overall (Reactor investigations and Reactor Assists to the NRC Staff) decreased by 13 percent, accompanied by an 11 percent decrease in reactor investigations and an 18 percent decrease in reactorrelated Assists to the NRC Staff. Materials investigations and Materials Assists to the NRC Staff, decreased overall, accompanied by a 36 percent decrease in materials investigations and a 36 percent decrease in materialsrelated Assists to the NRC Staff during the same period.

FIGURE 3 CASES CLOSED DURING FY 2007–2011 FOR THE REACTOR AND MATERIALS PROGRAMS

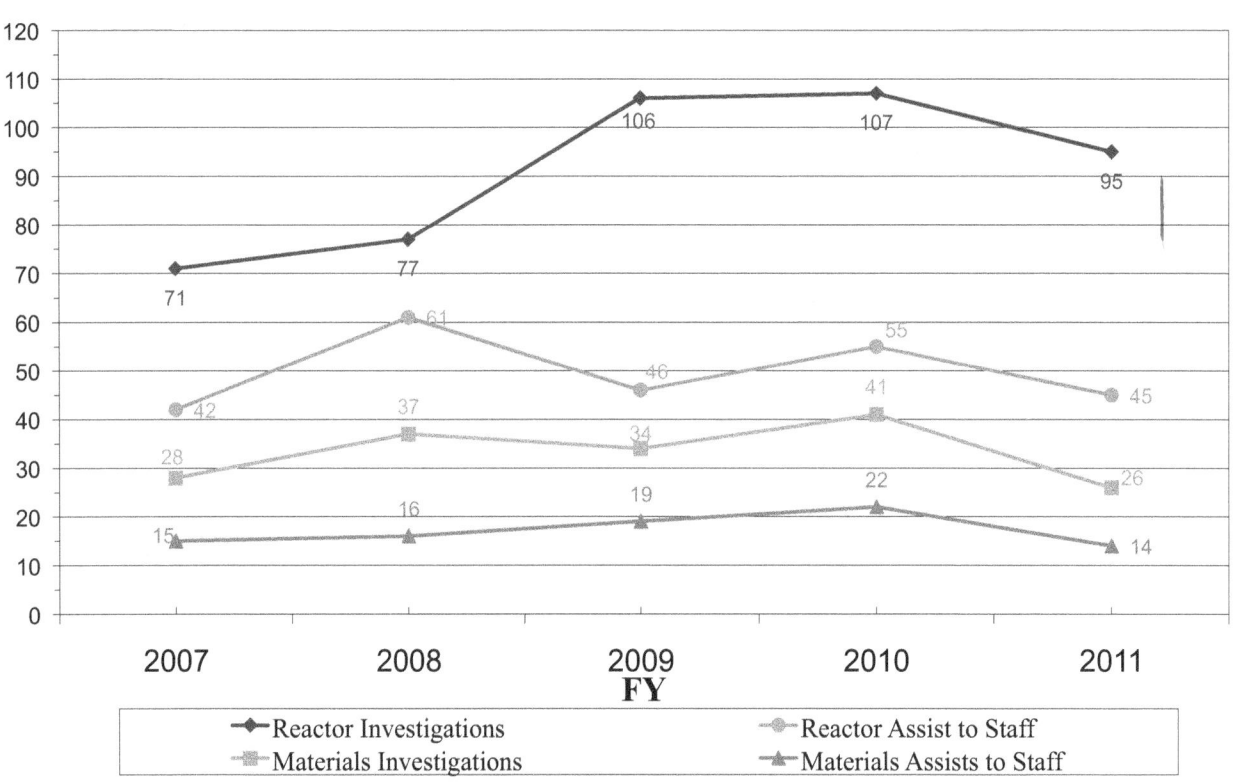

Of the 180 cases closed in FY 2011, 40 investigations were closed after OI substantiated willfulness on one or more of the allegations of wrongdoing, 77 investigations were closed after it did not substantiate willful wrongdoing, 4 investigations were closed administratively, and 59 investigations were Assists to the NRC Staff.

MANAGEMENT OF CASES

Figure 4 shows a decrease in the total casespecific staff hours (investigation) during FY 2010–2011 (from 36,000 to 28,000 investigative hours). Specifically, case activities in FY 2011 (planning, field work, and the analysis of information) decreased along with the hours toward case administration (Freedom of Information Act and other miscellaneous activities).

FIGURE 4 CASESPECIFIC STAFF HOURS

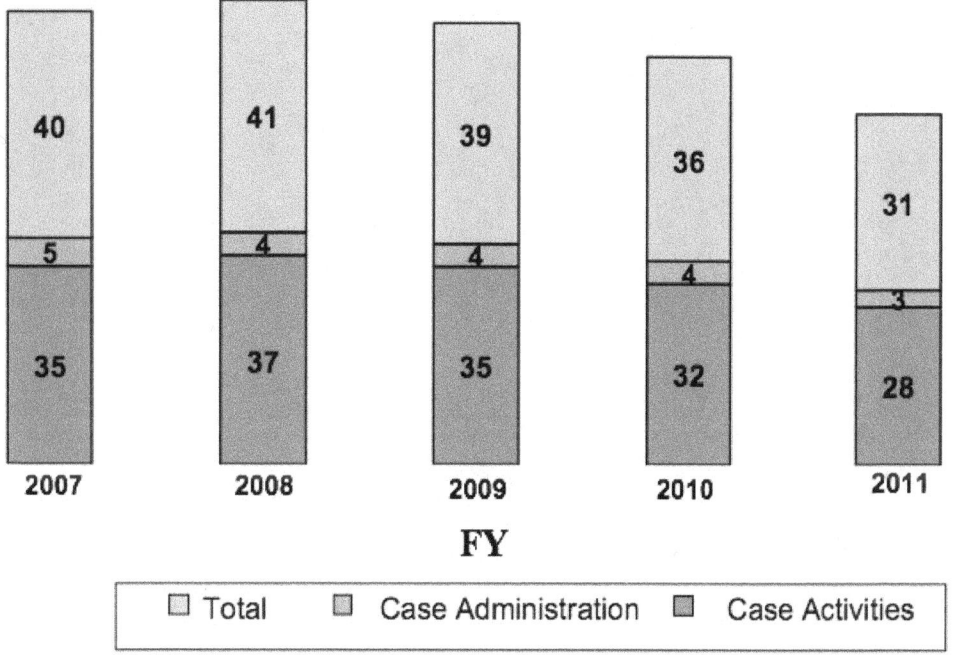

SIGNIFICANT INVESTIGATIONS

James A. Fitzpatrick Nuclear Power Plant

An OI investigation determined that a former radiation protection technician (RPT) at the James A. Fitzpatrick Nuclear Power Plant willfully prepared, signed, and submitted quantitative fit test records to an NRC licensee that were materially inaccurate. Beginning in 2006 and continuing through 2009, the former RPT submitted test records for approximately 32 employees that falsely documented that the employees successfully completed respirator fit tests when, in fact, no such tests had been conducted. This investigation was referred for prosecution to the Department of Justice (DOJ), U.S. Attorney's Office for the Northern District of New York. On September 8, 2011, the former RPT pleaded guilty to a one count information charging him with a felony violation of the Atomic Energy Act. On January 11, 2011, the former RPT was sentenced to one year of probation and fined $1,000. This matter remains under NRC regulatory review.

An OI investigation established that, on multiple occasions, an RPT deliberately violated NRC regulations and licensee procedures governing radiation protection by not completing radiation protection daily inspections or checks of highradiation area boundaries and related equipment. In addition, OI substantiated that the RPT deliberately falsified department surveillance and survey records on multiple occasions by initialing or signing records, or doing both, on behalf of another RPT for work that had not been done. This investigation was referred to DOJ for prosecution consideration and remains under NRC regulatory review.

St. Lucie Plant

An OI investigation substantiated that two RPTs engaged in deliberate misconduct by willfully falsifying health physics surveys at Florida Power and Light Company's St. Lucie Nuclear Plant. The licensee identified the falsified surveys after it compared the surveys to records generated by other technicians. Additionally, one RPT admitted bypassing the reader station turnstiles at the entrance to the radiation-controlled area many times and continued to bypass the turnstiles after being warned by a supervisor. This investigation was referred to DOJ for prosecution consideration. On March 25, 2011, the NRC issued a Severity Level IV non-cited violation to the licensee.

Paducah Gaseous Diffusion Plant

An OI investigation substantiated that a former operator employed by the U.S. Enrichment Corporation's Paducah Gaseous Diffusion Plant deliberately violated radiation protection procedures and technical safety requirements. The operator deliberately failed to adhere to radiation protection procedures by transporting a contaminated object from the contamination control zone to the operations monitoring room without following appropriate selfmonitoring procedures for radiological contamination. This failure to follow procedures led to contamination within other areas of the facility. This investigation was referred to DOJ for prosecution consideration. On August 17, 2011, the NRC issued a confirmatory order to the U.S. Enrichment Corporation Corporation to confirm commitments made resulting from an alternative dispute resolution settlement agreement.

S&R Engineering S.E.

This OI investigation substantiated that the President of S&R Engineering S.E. deliberately failed to provide complete and accurate information to the NRC on the location of a moisture density gauge. Evidence obtained during the investigation confirmed that the S&R Engineering S.E. President was in possession of the moisture density gauge despite the fact that he previously informed the NRC staff that the gauge had been transferred to another licensee. Additionally, the investigation determined that the S&R Engineering S.E. President deliberately failed to comply with a previously issued NRC order by not disposing of (transferring) the moisture density gauge in a proper and prescribed manner. This investigation was referred to DOJ for prosecution consideration. This matter remains under NRC regulatory review.

Cardinal Health

An OI investigation substantiated that a Technician II/radiation safety officer (RSO) deliberately removed extremity and body dosimetry badges while handling a chemical cartridge. The RSO admitted deliberately removing the badges while handling the cartridges on two separate occasions on the same day in violation of NRC regulations. This investigation was referred to DOJ for prosecution consideration. On November 9, 2011, the NRC issued a Severity Level III violation to Cardinal Health and a Severity Level III violation to the RSO.

Palisades Nuclear Plant

An OI investigation determined that an atthecontrols (ATC) reactor operator deliberately violated ATC procedures by improperly removing himself from his watchstanding responsibilities. The ATC reactor operator admitted leaving his station despite knowing that he had not been given proper turnover or approval from the control room supervisor. The ATC reactor operator further admitted leaving his station while the control room supervisor was telling him to stop. This investigation was referred to DOJ for prosecution consideration. The case remains under NRC regulatory review.

Palo Verde Nuclear Generating Station

An OI investigation substantiated that a former security officer (SO) was willfully inattentive while on duty. The OI investigation revealed that the SO was inattentive and asleep, which the SO admitted upon being questioned by OI. The OI investigation also determined that no mitigating factors existed and that the SO was acting on his own. The SO's employment has been terminated. This investigation was referred to DOJ for prosecution consideration. On May 9, 2011, the NRC issued a green non-cited violation to Palo Verde Nuclear Generating Station.

CPN International, Inc.

An OI investigation substantiated that CPN personnel willfully exported and attempted to export moisture density equipment to embargoed destinations in violation of NRC regulations. On three occasions, the customer service manager/former alternate RSO or the product manager/ RSO, or both, shipped or attempted to ship moisture density gauges to Iraq and the Sudan. The OI investigation revealed that both individuals had received training on embargoed destinations and the related NRC regulations. This investigation was referred to DOJ for prosecution consideration. It remains under NRC regulatory review.

Arkansas Nuclear One

An OI investigation determined that a security officer (SO) at the ANO plant deliberately falsified NRCrequired security logs. The SO did not perform two NRCrequired safety checks in violation of NRC regulations but reported that the checks had been completed. The SO admitted to not performing the security checks. An OI review of the records confirmed that the SO never entered the area in which the security checks were allegedly performed. Subsequently, the SO's employment was terminated and a record was placed in the Personnel Access Database System. This investigation was referred to DOJ for prosecution consideration. It remains under NRC regulatory review.

Accurate NDE and Inspection, LCLLC

An OI investigation substantiated that a radiographer deliberately violated operating procedures and NRC regulations by making an unauthorized attempt to retrieve a source that had become disconnected. The OI investigation revealed that Accurate NDE and Inspection, LLC, personnel were conducting radiographic operations on an unmanned production platform when the radiography source became disconnected. The licensee concluded that the source fell into the Gulf of Mexico during the unauthorized retrieval attempt. The OI investigation also determined that the same radiographer deliberately falsified the licensee's daily radiation report for the same date that the source was lost by providing inaccurate dosimeter readings in the report. This investigation was referred to DOJ for prosecution consideration. It remains under NRC regulatory review.

South Texas Project

OI substantiated that a contract carpenter employed by Stone and Webster for the South Texas Project willfully failed to report a felony arrest. The contractor admitted to OI that he falsified the personnel history questionnaire to gain unescorted access in 2007. In addition, following a court appearance in 2009, the contract carpenter continued to omit the disposition of the arrest on the personnel history questionnaire submitted for 2009–2010. The OI investigation disproved the contract carpenter's claims that omitting the arrest was based on advice received from an attorney and a judge. This investigation was referred to DOJ for prosecution consideration. On November 3, 2011, the NRC issued a Severity Level IV noncited violation to the South Texas Project.

San Onofre Nuclear Generating Station

The OI investigation substantiated that a radwaste operator at San Onofre Nuclear Generating Station willfully failed to perform auto tour rounds of the auxiliary building on 6 days between September and December 2009. The radwaste operator admitted to OI that the records of the auto tour rounds were falsified to reflect completion, and the evidence indicated that the radwaste operator did not enter or exit the only security door providing access to the area in which the rounds were to be conduct during the time when a "satisfactory" completion was recorded. With one exception, the OI investigation determined that no other operator performed the rounds as required. The radwaste operator's employment was terminated and a record was placed in the Personnel Access Database System. This investigation was referred to DOJ for prosecution consideration. On May 5, 2011, the NRC issued a Severity Level IV non-cited violation to San Onofre Nuclear Generating Station.

SIGNIFICANT ASSISTS TO THE NRC STAFF

Cooper Nuclear Station

OI initiated this Assist to the NRC Staff to determine whether Cooper Nuclear Station (CNS) received a substandard or fraudulent motoroperated valve from a contractor (parts vendor). The valve was purchased and shipped to CNS as new; however, a receipt inspection identified the valve as exhibiting signs of significant "wear and tear." OI seized the valve for further analysis. Based on information obtained from interviews, document examinations, and inspection activities, OI determined that the valve was in fact new. The valve exhibited signs of significant "wear and tear" caused by the conduct of rigorous testing to ensure that it met the performance and quality requirements identified by CNS.

NRC FORM 335 (12-2010) NRCMD 3.7	U.S. NUCLEAR REGULATORY COMMISSION	1. REPORT NUMBER (Assigned by NRC, Add Vol., Supp., Rev., and Addendum Numbers, if any.)
	BIBLIOGRAPHIC DATA SHEET *(See instructions on the reverse)*	NUREG 1830, Vol. 8

2. TITLE AND SUBTITLE	3. DATE REPORT PUBLISHED	
Office of Investigations Annual Report FY 2011	MONTH	YEAR
	February	2012
	4. FIN OR GRANT NUMBER	

5. AUTHOR(S)	6. TYPE OF REPORT
	Annual
	7. PERIOD COVERED *(Inclusive Dates)*
	10/01/2010 to 9/30/2011

8. PERFORMING ORGANIZATION - NAME AND ADDRESS *(If NRC, provide Division, Office or Region, U.S. Nuclear Regulatory Commission, and mailing address; if contractor, provide name and mailing address.)*

Office of Investigations
U.S. Nuclear Regulatory Commission
Washington, DC 20555-0001

9. SPONSORING ORGANIZATION - NAME AND ADDRESS *(If NRC, type "Same as above"; if contractor, provide NRC Division, Office or Region, U.S. Nuclear Regulatory Commission, and mailing address.)*

Same

10. SUPPLEMENTARY NOTES

11. ABSTRACT *(200 words or less)*

This report describes Office of Investigations case activities during FY 2011.

12. KEY WORDS/DESCRIPTORS *(List words or phrases that will assist researchers in locating the report.)*	13. AVAILABILITY STATEMENT
Office of Investigations FY 2011 Annual	unlimited
	14. SECURITY CLASSIFICATION
	(This Page)
	unclassified
	(This Report)
	unclassified
	15. NUMBER OF PAGES
	16. PRICE

NRC FORM 335 (12-2010)

NUREG-1830, Vol. 8

February 2012

www.ingramcontent.com/pod-product-compliance
Lightning Source LLC
Chambersburg PA
CBHW080357290526
45791CB00009BA/2906